OXFORD BOO

Human Interest

Nobody Listens

ROWENA WAKEFIELD

Stage 1 (400 headwords)

Illustrated by Pascal Campion

Series Editor: Rachel Bladon
Founder Editors: Jennifer Bassett
and Tricia Hedge

UNIVERSITY PRESS

Great Clarendon Street, Oxford, OX2 6DP, United Kingdom

Oxford University Press is a department of the University of Oxford.
It furthers the University's objective of excellence in research, scholarship,
and education by publishing worldwide. Oxford is a registered trade
mark of Oxford University Press in the UK and in certain other countries

© Oxford University Press 2016

The moral rights of the author have been asserted

First published in Oxford Bookworms 2016

10 9 8 7 6 5 4

No unauthorized photocopying

All rights reserved. No part of this publication may be reproduced,
stored in a retrieval system, or transmitted, in any form or by any means,
without the prior permission in writing of Oxford University Press, or as
expressly permitted by law, by licence or under terms agreed with the
appropriate reprographics rights organization. Enquiries concerning
reproduction outside the scope of the above should be sent to the ELT
Rights Department, Oxford University Press, at the address above

You must not circulate this work in any other form and you must
impose this same condition on any acquirer

Links to third party websites are provided by Oxford in good faith and
for information only. Oxford disclaims any responsibility for the materials
contained in any third party website referenced in this work

ISBN: 978 0 19 420951 9
A complete audio recording of this Bookworms edition
of *Nobody Listens* is available.

Printed in China

Word count (main text): 5,347

For more information on the Oxford Bookworms Library,
visit www.oup.com/elt/gradedreaders

ACKNOWLEDGEMENTS

Cover Photo: Getty Images (young man on phone/Hero Images)

Cover Illustration: Simon Reid

Story illustrations by: Pascal Campion/Shannon Associates

The publisher would like to thank the following for permission to reproduce photographs:
Getty Images pp.57 (photographer Brandon Stanton/STAN HONDA),
57 (Rebecca Black/Allen Berezovsky), cover (young man on phone/Hero Images).

CONTENTS

1	Birthday	1
2	Bella	4
3	Lesson	12
4	Video	20
5	"Likes"	26
6	Song	35
7	Smile	40

GLOSSARY	42
ACTIVITIES: Before Reading	44
ACTIVITIES: While Reading	45
ACTIVITIES: After Reading	50
ACTIVITIES: Discussion	56
ACTIVITIES: Project	57
ABOUT THE BOOKWORMS LIBRARY	60

CHAPTER 1
BIRTHDAY

My name is Alex and today is my fifteenth birthday. Nobody says "Happy Birthday" to me because nobody at my school knows about my birthday. They don't know me. I started at this school two weeks ago because we moved here for my mom and dad's work.

We're always moving to different towns and I'm always going to new schools. When I was younger, I made new friends every time. But we're always leaving and I'm always losing them. When I leave, people forget me. I don't want to start again and again. So I don't make new friends now. It's easier.

Today at school, I have a computer lesson. It's OK. I like computers, but I like watching music videos best. I feel happy when I listen to music. I can forget about everything. The best music website is VideoSpace. It has lots of music videos – by famous singers and by new singers.

The computer teacher is nice. I finish my work quickly, so she says, "Alex, you can watch some music videos now." Maybe *she* knows about my birthday.

After the computer lesson, I eat my lunch. Nobody sits with me. Then I have another lesson, and after that I go home. When I get in, the house is quiet. I don't have any brothers or sisters, and my mom and dad aren't home because they're working.

On the table is a note. It says:

Happy Birthday, son! We're sorry, Alex, but we have an important meeting, so we're going to be home late. This is your birthday present.

Love, Mom and Dad XXX

"We're sorry, Alex, but we have an important meeting."

Birthday 3

A meeting! My mom and dad are always in meetings with important people. They talk about "important things" and make lots of money. But I don't understand it. Why do they need more money? We have a big house, an expensive car. Why do we need more? It's my birthday! I want them *here*.

Next to the note, there's a big present. I open it. It's a guitar, a very expensive guitar. I asked my mom and dad for it. It's really cool. At first, I can't stop looking at it. I love it. I want to talk about it with my mom and dad. I want to play it for them. But there's nobody here. I start playing a song on the guitar. It's my new song: I wrote it last week.

Everybody is far away
Only me
Day after day.

Nobody listens and they don't hear
Look at me
I'm standing here.

Why does everything feel so wrong?
My one friend
Is you, this song.

CHAPTER 2
BELLA

It's Saturday. No school! I get out of bed and go downstairs. My mom is sitting at the kitchen table. She's working on her laptop. She sees me and says, "Morning, Alex. Do you like your guitar?"

I say, "I love it. Thank you. It's amazing."

"Good," my mom says. "What are you going to do today?"

"I have some homework, and then I'm going to play my guitar. I want to write a new song."

"That's nice. Dad is at work all day and I'm working here. I need to call some people. But tonight, let's have a birthday dinner for you. We can go to a restaurant – you, me, and Dad." She smiles, and then she looks at her laptop.

I have breakfast, and go into the next room and get my new guitar. I play a song. It's a song by an American singer. I saw the video on VideoSpace and loved it, so I learned to play it on the guitar. It's a fast, happy song. It's about love.

Our love is alive
Our love is free
Our love is always
You and me.

But then my mom calls from the kitchen: "Alex! Can you do that in your room, please? I'm working."

I wanted my mom to hear the song. I wanted her to listen to *me*. But she's not interested in me. I'm not her work.

I run up to my room noisily and shut the door. I'm angry and I want her to know. It's hot, so I open a window, and then I play the song again.

I play the song again.

When I finish the song, I hear clapping from outside. Is it my mom? Did she hear me and come and listen? I go to the window, but there's nobody in the yard. I can't see into the yard next door because there are lots of trees. Was somebody there? I listen for a minute, but everything is quiet.

I don't like it. I close the window and take some homework out of my backpack, but I can't stop thinking about that clapping. Who was it? Did somebody hear me? I can't do my homework. I sit at my laptop and watch videos on VideoSpace. Maybe I can learn another new song. But I'm thinking about that clapping. Who was it?

Someone comes to the door, and my mom calls up to me. "Alex! There's somebody here for you."

Who is it? I don't have any friends. Nobody knows me. I think of the clapping. Is this because of the song? I feel sick. I go downstairs, but I don't want to.

There's a girl there. She's fourteen or fifteen. Her hair is long and brown, and she has big blue eyes. She's beautiful... and she's smiling at me. I can't speak. What can I say to a girl like this?

"Hi! I'm Bella," she says.

"Hi," I say, in a small voice. She waits for a minute, and then I say, "I'm Alex."

"Hi, Alex!" She laughs. "I live next door to you."

Bella

She's beautiful... and she's smiling at me.

A beautiful girl is talking to me – and she lives in the house next door!

"You go to my school," she says. "You're new, right?"

"Yes."

"Cool. So, was that you with the guitar?"

The clapping. I open my mouth. I can't speak.

"I heard a guitar. Was it you?" she says again.

"Oh... Well, yes."

"It was a really cool song. And you're an amazing guitar player."

I can't believe it. She liked it! This beautiful girl liked my music! I start saying something, but it doesn't come out right.

"Th...Th...Thanks."

"I love the guitar, but I can't play."

"Oh?"

What's wrong with me? Why can't I say something interesting, something more than "Oh"?

"But I want to learn," says Bella.

"You do?"

"Yes." She looks at me carefully, and then she says, "You're really good! Can you teach me?"

I think, no! No, I can't teach you! I want to teach you, but I can't talk to you because you're beautiful and I'm me. But I say, "I can play the guitar, but I don't teach it. I'm not a teacher."

"Oh, that doesn't matter," she says happily. "Maybe

I can watch you when you're playing, and you can help me."

"Well, I don't know…" I say, but she looks at me with her big blue eyes, and says, "Oh, please! Let's try it! Are you free tonight?"

I can't play the guitar in front of this beautiful girl, I think. What am I going to do? And then I remember. "I can't. Sorry. I'm having a birthday dinner with my mom and dad tonight."

"A birthday dinner? Is it your birthday today?"

"Yesterday."

"Happy Birthday! Did you get any nice presents?"

"A new guitar."

"Amazing! Well, Alex, can you give me your phone number? Then I can text you. Maybe you can teach me the guitar another time."

I can't say no, so I give her my phone number.

"Bye, Alex," she says.

"Bye," I say, and I close the door.

Two hours later, I get a text from Bella:

> Hi, Alex! It's Bella. Can you teach me guitar tomorrow night? Are you free at 7 o'clock? 😊

What am I going to do? People like me can't be friends with people like Bella. I need to think of an excuse. I text back:

> Hi. I have to do a lot of homework for Monday. Sorry. 😔

She replies:

> That's OK. Monday, after school? 🙂

What can I say? Another excuse?

> Sorry, Bella. I'm going to the movies on Monday. 😔

She replies:

> Cool. What are you going to see? Tuesday?

I don't reply for a minute. I can't make more excuses. I get another text from Bella:

> Tuesday? 5 o'clock?

OK, Alex, here goes…

> Cool. See you on Tuesday.

> See you on Tuesday! B x 😊

In three days, beautiful Bella is coming to my house. She wants to play the guitar and listen to me… What am I going to do?

What am I going to do?

CHAPTER 3
LESSON

It's Tuesday. Bella is going to be here in thirty minutes. I feel really sick. I saw her at school today, but she didn't see me. She has lots of friends. She isn't going to like me, I know it. I'm quiet, and I'm not interesting, and she's going to see that. I don't feel good.

She isn't going to like me, I know it.

And then it's five o'clock and Bella is here, at my house. She's smiling and she's beautiful.

"Hi, Alex! How are you?"

"OK. How are you?"

"I'm really good, thanks. How was your birthday dinner?"

"OK, thanks."

"Did you finish your homework?"

"Yes."

"And how was the movie?"

"It was OK."

We stand and nobody talks.

"Can I come in, Alex?" she says.

"Yes, sorry. Come in."

Nice one, Alex, I think. A beautiful girl comes to your house and you forget to ask her in.

She comes with me into the kitchen. She's in my house!

"I'm really excited about learning the guitar. Is it easy? Can you teach me some songs?" She stops, and laughs. "Sorry. I can't stop talking. My mom is always telling me that. Can I see your new guitar?"

She smiles. I really like her smile. She sits down, and I get my guitar, and show it to her.

"This guitar is amazing, Alex."

"Thanks."

"What did you play before this one?" she asks.

I show her my old guitar. "I played this for years."

"So you have two guitars?" Bella says. "Cool!"

That smile! I can't stop looking at her.

"So," she says, "can we start?"

"OK," I say. "Do you want to learn on my new guitar?"

"Oh no, Alex," she says. "I can't! Not on your new one!"

"OK, then," I say, and I give her my old guitar. "This is a nice guitar, too. And better for learning."

"So what do I do first?" Bella asks. "How do I hold it? Like this?"

"No. OK, you need to put your left hand here."

"Here?" she says.

"Yes, that's good. Now put your right hand here."

"Like this?"

"Yes."

"I'm going to show you three chords," I say. I take my new guitar, play three chords, and then look at Bella. "Now you try."

"I'm sorry, Alex, I need to go slower than that. Can you start with one chord?"

"OK, sorry. Try this one."

I show her the chord and she watches me. Then she tries it on my old guitar.

"Is that it?" she asks.

"Um, no."

"Show me again."

Lesson 15

"*Show me again.*"

I play the chord again. Bella watches my hands. Then she tries.

"Is this right?"

It's wrong. I move her hand.

"Try now," I say.

She tries the chord.

"I did it!"

She's smiling. She plays it again.

"Good," I say. "Now, try another one."

After fifteen minutes, Bella can play three chords, so I teach her a song. The song only has those three chords. She plays it. It's not amazing, but it's OK.

"You're a really good teacher, Alex. I can't believe it! I can play a song. OK, I'm going to play it again."

She plays the song again. It's better this time.

"You're good," I say.

"Thanks! I love it. It's difficult, but I love it. When did you start playing?"

"When I was five years old."

"Five? Really? That's very young."

"My dad had a guitar and one day I started playing it. And I never stopped!"

"Did you take lessons?"

"Yes. I took lessons at first, but then we moved, so I stopped. After that, I learned from books and videos."

"That's really cool. And now you're teaching me!"

"I'm trying," I laugh.

"You're a good teacher. What music do you like?"

"I love all music: old, new, everything," I say. "I listen to my dad's music, and I like watching new music on VideoSpace."

"Cool. I love some of the bands on VideoSpace."

"Can I show you something?" I say.

"Of course," says Bella.

I get my laptop and I open VideoSpace. I find a video of FLY. They're amazing. Bella looks at me, excited. She says, "You know FLY?"

"I *love* FLY. They're cool."

"I love FLY, too," she says. She likes FLY! I can't believe it!

"Look at this!" I say, and I put the laptop in front of Bella on the table. "Watch the guitar player now. He's amazing! I want to play like that one day."

Bella is watching me, but she isn't talking. She's listening.

"I love their new song, too," I say. "They're playing near here next year, I think. I really want to see them. Oh, listen to that voice! Now that's cool!"

Bella smiles and says, "You're different when you talk about music, Alex."

"Different?"

"You're usually quiet, but when you talk about music you're... more alive. We have to put a video of you on VideoSpace!"

"We have to put a video of you on VideoSpace!"

"What?" I say, and suddenly I feel sick. "Me? Put a video of me on VideoSpace? No. I don't want to. I don't play for people."

"Why not?"

"I don't know."

"But you're really good."

"I'm OK. *FLY* are really good."

"No, Alex, when I heard you on Saturday, it was amazing. Your music is really good, and people want to hear music like that. You *have* to put something on VideoSpace."

Lesson

"I don't want to," I say. "Forget it."

She looks at me with her big blue eyes. "OK," she says, "but please think about it."

"Perhaps," I say.

Then Bella smiles. "Can we look at some more videos on VideoSpace?"

We do. We look at some more bands. We like all the same music. It's cool.

Bella is really interesting. She loves soccer, and she teaches it to seven- and eight-year-olds. She tells me all about it. And then suddenly it's seven o'clock and she says, "I have to go now, Alex. Thank you for the lesson. I loved it."

I don't want her to go home. I liked teaching her and I really liked talking to her. I don't usually talk to people. I talk to my mom and dad sometimes, when they're at home, but that's different. I can't talk to my mom and dad about FLY. I really want to see her again, but how do I ask?

Then she says, "Can we have another lesson, Alex? Tomorrow?"

She wants another lesson!

"Yes. OK," I say. "What time?"

"After my soccer practice, seven o'clock?"

"Cool," I say. "See you tomorrow."

"See you tomorrow. Thanks, Alex."

And she leaves.

CHAPTER 4
VIDEO

Bella comes the next day, and the day after. She comes every day for a week. We talk about music and watch the best bands on VideoSpace. We play the guitar and we laugh and have a good time. I like her. I like her a lot. She's interesting and she's beautiful. She's my friend. I have a friend! It feels good. Is she more than a friend? No! Is she? I don't know.

But why am I thinking about this? My family never stays in the same town for more than a year. I'm going to make friends with Bella, and then my mom and dad are going to say, "Sorry, Alex, we're moving." But I don't want to say goodbye again. Not to Bella.

On Tuesday night, a week after our first lesson, Bella asks, "Can you play me a song?"

"What?"

"I want you to play."

Sometimes I play some chords because I'm showing Bella something, but usually I teach and she plays.

"I don't know," I say.

"Go on, Alex. One song!"

Me? Play for Bella? Nobody listens to my music. My mom and dad do, sometimes, but no one from school. I play for me.

"Please, Alex!" Bella says.

Video   21

"Why?"

"You're really good, and I want to listen to you," she says. "You always listen to me. Play the new FLY song. You can play it – you told me yesterday."

I think about it for a second or two.

"Please, please, please, Alex!"

So I say yes, because I want Bella to be happy. It's only one song. I take my guitar and play her the FLY song. I think about the music, and for a minute or two I forget about everything, and sing and play. Well, nearly everything. I don't forget about Bella, and when the song ends, she smiles and claps.

"Amazing, Alex!"

I smile. It feels OK, playing for Bella.

"Can you play me one of *your* songs, too?" she asks.

"You said one song!"

"I know, but I really want to hear one of your songs."

I look at her and I can't say no.

"OK."

I play it, and Bella loves it. "Alex, play it again," she says. "But this time, can I take a video of you on my phone?"

"What?"

"I want to take a video of you!"

"Why?" I say.

"Because I love the song and I want to listen to it at home."

I don't want to say no to Bella, but I really don't like this idea.

"Go on, Alex!"

"I don't know, Bella."

"Please, please, please, please, please, please…"

"Oh, OK!" I say. "For you."

She's smiling and laughing. I play the song again and she records it. I don't like being in front of a camera, but a voice in my head is saying, "Bella wants a video of me!"

"Bella wants a video of me!"

Video 23

After the lesson, Bella leaves. I think about her with a video of me on her phone and I smile. I get my guitar and I start writing a new song. This one is about Bella.

* * *

It's seven o'clock on Wednesday morning, and I'm in bed. I look at my phone. I have four texts from Bella, and they all say "Call me!" I call her.

"Hi, Bella. Are you OK?"

"Yes, yes. Are you at home?"

She's excited, and she's speaking very fast.

"Yes. Why?"

"Can I come to your house?" she says.

"Now?"

"Yes! Now!"

"OK," I say. "I need ten minutes. I'm in bed."

"OK. See you in ten minutes."

I don't understand. What's this all about? I get up, and ten minutes later, Bella arrives at the door. She's excited.

"Last night, I put your video on VideoSpace!" she says.

"What video?"

"The video of your song! From last night!"

"What?"

"The song – I put it on VideoSpace," she says again.

"You did what?"

I feel sick. I can't speak. Me? On VideoSpace?

"Look, Alex!" says Bella, and she takes her phone from her pocket.

But I don't look. "Why did you do that?!" I say.

I'm angry, and Bella can hear it in my voice. She looks up from her phone.

"That video was for you, Bella," I say. "It wasn't for VideoSpace."

"I know, but—"

"No, that video was for you! Only you. Why did you do this?"

"I wanted people to see it," Bella says. "I wanted to help you."

"But you didn't ask me!"

"I know, but—"

"I didn't want people to see it," I say.

"But—"

"I can't believe this, Bella," I say.

"I did it because you're really good," she says. "People need to hear your music!"

"It's MY music. That song was for you."

"I'm sorry, I—"

"Sorry?" I say. "You did it and you didn't ask me. That is not OK!"

"But—"

"No, Bella. That song was NOT for VideoSpace. It was for you." And I run upstairs to my room, and leave Bella at the door.

"That song was NOT for VideoSpace. It was for you."

CHAPTER 5
"LIKES"

When I walk to school that morning, I can't stop thinking. Why did Bella put my song on VideoSpace? How could she do that to me? I look at my phone, and there's a text from her. It's a link. It's a link to the video of me on VideoSpace. I feel sick. I can't watch it.

When I arrive at school, people are looking at me and talking. Why are they looking at me? What are they saying?

I have a computer lesson first, and when I go into the classroom, a boy walks past me and says, "I saw your video, Alex."

"What?"

But the teacher arrives, and the boy goes and sits at his computer. He saw the video? The video on VideoSpace? No! How? This isn't happening. Please! I watch the boy. He's talking to the boy next to him. They stop talking and they look at me. I feel sick. I want to leave the lesson. Now other people are looking at me and talking. After this lesson, I'm going to run out of school, I think. I'm going to leave and never come back.

At the end of the lesson, I want to go, but the teacher says, "Alex! Can you wait for a minute, please?"

Everyone goes, and she comes and sits next to me.

"Likes"

I'm going to leave and never come back.

"Alex, is everything OK?"

"Yes, Miss King," I say.

"You weren't very happy about something today," she says.

"I'm OK, Miss King," I say.

"Well, when you need to, you can talk to me. Any time," she says.

"Thanks, Miss King," I say. "Can I go now?"

"Yes, Alex. See you tomorrow."

I leave the classroom, but some of the boys from my lesson are waiting outside. They're looking at one boy's phone. I can hear my voice. They're watching the video. They all look up. Nobody speaks.

Then the boy with the phone says, "Cool video, Alex."

Another boy says, "Yeah, really cool."

What? They like it?

"You have 621 'likes'!" the first boy says. "When I put my video on VideoSpace, only five people watched it!"

"621 'likes'?" I say.

"622 now!" he says. "Look! And lots of comments, too. All good."

He shows me his phone, and I read some of the comments quickly:

> Amazing song! Love this!
> More videos, please!
> Cool music.
> Your voice is REALLY good.
> Did you write this song? I love it!
> Record another one!

"Likes" 29

"You have 621 'likes'!"

I can't believe it: people like my music. The boys from my school like my music. And 622 people – no, 624! It feels amazing. I give the boy his phone.

And now I understand: Bella came to my house this morning because she wanted to tell me about this. And I was angry with her! I was angry because I was afraid, but people don't hate my music. They like it. I feel really bad. Bella wanted to help me. I need to talk to her.

The coolest one of the boys says, "Alex, some of us are playing at the youth club tomorrow. Do you want to come and play your guitar? It's a music night. It's going to be cool."

I think for a second or two. Do I want to? Do I want to play in front of people? The boys are all watching me. I can't say no now.

"OK."

I can't believe it. I'm going to play my guitar at the youth club, in front of people! Is that really a good idea? But I can't think about that now. I need to talk to Bella.

I look for her all day at school, but I don't see her. When I get home, I send her a text:

> Bella, I saw the video and the comments. I understand, and I'm really sorry.

I wait. One minute. No reply. Five minutes. No reply. Thirty minutes. An hour.

I send another text:

> I'm sorry, Bella. Please reply!

I want to see her. I want to talk to her. Is she home? I start walking to her house, but then I stop. Maybe she's angry with me. Maybe she doesn't want to reply. Maybe she's never going to reply. Bella, please, please reply. I'm sorry. I don't want to lose you.

Then suddenly I remember! It's Wednesday. Bella has soccer practice. It's OK. She isn't replying because she's teaching soccer. Her practice ends at six thirty, and it's five o'clock now, so I go home and look at VideoSpace on my laptop. 708 "likes" now. I play some music videos, and look at my watch. Five fifteen. Come on, Bella.

The time goes slowly. Five thirty. Five fifty. I open a book, but I can't read it. Six o'clock. Six fifteen. I look at my homework, but I can't think.

It's six thirty. Her soccer practice ends now. It's going to be OK. Please be OK.

"Alex! Dinner!"

It's my mom. I'm not hungry, but I go downstairs. I put my phone on the table. I don't want to eat. Text me, Bella! Please text me. I sit at the table with my mom and dad, but I can't eat.

My dad asks, "How was school, Alex?"

"OK."

I look at my phone. No texts.

"Do you like this school, Alex?"

"It's OK."

I look at my phone again.

"Are the teachers nice?"

I can't stop looking at my phone.

"They're OK."

Still no text.

I can't stop looking at my phone.

"Do you have some nice friends?"

I don't answer. Then my mom starts asking questions, too.

"Bella from next door is your friend, isn't she? She's a nice girl."

"I don't want to talk about Bella."

I look at my phone.

My dad says, "Alex! Stop looking at your phone. We're eating, and we're talking to you."

I eat, but I don't talk. I don't want to. After dinner, I go to my bedroom. I need to talk to Bella. I look at my watch. It's seven ten. She isn't playing soccer now. She's at home. But there's no text from her. OK, I'm going to her house. I open our front door and then I see her. Bella is there, in the street. She's walking to my house. We start speaking at the same time.

"Alex, I'm sorry! I wanted to help."

"Bella, I'm sorry."

"No, I was wrong," Bella says.

"You weren't. You were right."

We laugh.

"793 people 'like' your music, Alex!"

"804!" I say. "Come and have a look on my laptop."

We go up to my room and look at VideoSpace.

"813 now!" says Bella. "Amazing! Look at the comments, Alex. They love you! They want more videos."

"I know." I tell her about the boy from my lesson, and the youth club tomorrow.

"That's really cool!" she says. "Can I come and watch?"

"You *have* to come," I say. "I can't do it without you."

She smiles. "Do you want to put another video on VideoSpace?"

"Yes. No. I don't know. Maybe."

"Do it! Everybody loves you."

This is cool. People like my music and Bella is here. Everything is good. The best. We start talking about my songs. We're excited and talking fast. We talk about the next song, and about the youth club tomorrow. Then suddenly Bella kisses me. I can't believe it. I never kissed a girl before. I want to kiss Bella, but I'm really afraid. I stand up. I don't kiss her. I can't kiss her. For a second or two, she says nothing, and then she runs out of the room. I can't believe it. Why did I *do* that?

Why did I do *that?*

CHAPTER 6
SONG

It's the next day, and I'm at school and I feel really bad. Last night, I texted Bella, but she didn't reply. Does she hate me? I'm sorry, Bella. Please understand! It wasn't you; it was me. I like you. You're amazing.

When I get home, my mom says, "I need to talk to you." And suddenly I know. It's happening again. We're moving. I know it. She always tells me like this.

"I don't want to talk, Mom."

"Alex, this is important."

I don't want to move! Why are we always moving? I want to be here. I want to be with Bella.

My mom says, "Alex, do you like it here?"

"What?"

"Do you like it? Do you like the house? Do you have friends? Is school OK?"

I don't reply. I'm thinking about Bella. I don't want to lose her.

For a minute, no one speaks, and then my mom says, "Alex, we're not going to move again. Dad and I want to stay here. But we need to know: are you happy here?"

What? I can't believe it.

"We're not moving?" I say.

"No, Alex. We're staying here. Do you want to stay?"

"Yes. Yes, I do."

This is amazing.

"You like it here?" my mom says.

"Yes, I like it."

"Good," she says.

I'm sitting and thinking: we aren't moving! We're staying. "That's cool, Mom," I say, and she smiles.

"Is Bella coming here tonight?" she asks.

"No," I say. "I'm playing some songs at the youth club. It's a music night. Some boys from my school are going."

"That's wonderful, Alex," she says. "Is Bella going?"

She has to, I think. She has to be there. I can't do it without her.

"I don't know," I say.

Mom looks at me and says, "She was crying last night when she went home. Is everything OK?"

I don't reply.

Mom waits, and then she says, "We all say the wrong thing sometimes, or do the wrong thing. And when we do, we need to say sorry."

I think, how? Or maybe I say it, because my mom says, "You're always writing songs, Alex. Say it with a song."

And I think, yes, she's right! A song. My song about Bella.

"Thanks, Mom," I say, and I kiss her.

"I don't know," I say.

I go to my room and get my guitar, and then I put my phone on a chair. I start recording. Then I sit in front of the chair and sing. I sing the song about Bella.

I sing the song about Bella.

Then came winter
Then I was cold
Everything was far
Nobody to hold

Now summer is here
Everything's new
The sun is out
Because I found you.

After the song, I say, "Bella, I'm sorry. This song is for you." Then I put the song on VideoSpace and send the link to her.

"Alex?"

It's my mom. She's standing outside my bedroom.

"Yes, Mom?"

"Is that a new song?"

"Yes."

"It's beautiful."

"Thanks."

And I feel good, because Mom listened to my song and she liked it. Is Bella going to like it, too?

CHAPTER 7
SMILE

I feel sick. I'm at the youth club and a band is playing. And I'm playing in ten minutes. There are lots of people there, and they're going to watch me and listen to me. Please like it, everybody!

Bella didn't reply to my text. I look for her, but she isn't here. Did she like the song? Maybe she's never going to speak to me again. I don't want to play my music. I want to go home. I want to leave. But then the music stops. I hear a voice.

"Thank you, everybody! Now, we have something new. Many of you saw his video on VideoSpace. Tonight we have Alex!"

Everybody is clapping. I stand in front of them. There are nearly a hundred people. They are all looking at me. They stop clapping. Nobody speaks. I want to be sick. But I can't leave now. And so I sing.

I start playing a song. I finish and everybody claps. I'm feeling better now. And then I see Bella. She's here! She's smiling the biggest smile. We're going to be OK. I know it. I look at her and I say, "This song's for Bella."

Then I play the song about her. I finish the song and everybody is clapping. I feel amazing. I did it! I put my guitar down, walk to Bella, and kiss her.

Bella's here! She's smiling the biggest smile.

GLOSSARY

amazing *(adj)* very interesting and different
another *(det)* one more
backpack *(n)* a big bag; you carry it on your back
band *(n)* a music group
believe *(v)* to think that something is true
birthday *(n)* the day when you were born
chord *(n)* two or more musical notes (sounds) played at the same time
clap *(v)* to make a noise with your hands, usually because you like something
comment *(n)* what you say/write to show what you think about something
cool *(adj)* great, amazing; fashionable and different
excuse *(n)* what you say to explain why you can't/didn't do something
hold *(v)* to have something in your hand or arms
idea *(n)* a plan or new thought
kiss *(v)* to touch somebody with your lips to show love
kitchen *(n)* a room; you cook food there
laptop *(n)* a small computer; you can carry it with you
lesson *(n)* a time when you learn something with a teacher
link *(n)* an address on a computer; it takes you to a website
maybe *(adv)* perhaps
meeting *(n)* a time when people meet, usually to talk about something
music *(n)* You make music when you sing or play instruments, e.g. the piano.
next door *(adv)* in or to the nearest house
note *(n)* a short letter

Glossary

outside *(adv)* not in a building or room

practice *(n)* when you do something many times because you want to do it well

present *(n)* something nice that you give to someone on a special day, e.g. their birthday

really *(adv)* very or very much

record *(v)* to make a video on a DVD, CD, or phone

reply *(v & n)* to answer

same *(adj)* not different

send *(v)* When you send something, e.g. a letter or a text, it goes to somebody in another place.

show *(v)* to help somebody to see something

sick *(adj)* not well

sing *(v)* to make music with your voice

song *(n)* music with words

take lessons *(v)* to learn something with a teacher

text *(n & v)* a note that you send by phone

try *(v)* begin to do something when you don't know how to do it or if you can

voice *(n)* the sound when you speak or sing

youth club *(n)* a meeting place for young people

ACTIVITIES

Before Reading

1 **Choose the correct words to complete these sentences.**

   band   birthday   clap   lesson   sick   song

   1 I really like the _____ *You've got a friend.*
   2 He didn't eat his dinner because he felt _____.
   3 When Izzy finished speaking, everyone started to _____.
   4 I'm going out with some friends tomorrow because it's my _____.
   5 In our English _____ today, we learned the English names for different animals.
   6 The Beatles were a famous _____ in the 1960s.

2 **Look at the front and back cover of the book. Are these sentences true or false?**

   1 This is a love story.
   2 Alex has a lot of friends.
   3 Alex plays the guitar.
   4 Alex likes playing music to lots of people.
   5 Alex's family moved to their house a long time ago.

ACTIVITIES

While Reading

Read Chapter 1. Then correct the <u>underlined</u> word in each sentence to make the sentences true.

1 Alex has a <u>music</u> lesson today.
2 Alex likes the <u>soccer</u> website VideoSpace.
3 At lunchtime, <u>the computer teacher</u> sits with Alex.
4 On the table next to the present, there is a <u>book</u>.
5 Alex's present from his mom and dad is a <u>computer</u>.

Answer these questions about Alex with *yes* or *no*.

1 Does he like his computer teacher?
2 Does he have any brothers or sisters?
3 Do his parents have a lot of money?
4 Does he sing a happy song?

Read Chapter 2. Write *B* (Bella) or *A* (Alex).

Who…
1 claps outside?
2 says, "I'm not a teacher"?
3 is not free tonight?
4 asks for a phone number?
5 wants to meet tomorrow night?
6 makes a lot of excuses?

ACTIVITIES: *While Reading*

Which three sentences are true? Check (✓) the three true sentences.

1 Alex wants his parents to have more time for him.
2 Bella came to Alex's house because she heard his song.
3 Alex wrote an unhappy song.
4 Alex doesn't like Bella.
5 Alex is going to the movies on Monday.

Choose the correct words to complete the sentences.

clapping   laptop   next door   song   text

1 Alex's mom is working on her _____.
2 Alex wants to write a new _____.
3 When Alex finishes playing, he hears _____.
4 Bella lives _____ to Alex.
5 Bella's first _____ says, "Can you teach me guitar tomorrow night?"

Read Chapter 3. Choose the best word to complete the questions, and then answer them.

How many   What   When   Which   Who

1 _____ guitars does Alex have?
2 _____ did Alex start playing the guitar?
3 _____ band do Bella and Alex like?
4 _____ does Bella want to put on VideoSpace?
5 _____ teaches soccer to young children?

Are the sentences true, false, or not mentioned in the story?

1 Bella doesn't want to learn on Alex's new guitar.
2 Alex never took guitar lessons when he was younger.
3 Bella's mom wants her to learn the guitar.
4 Bella doesn't like old music.
5 Alex and Bella like all the same music.
6 Bella can't have a guitar lesson on Wednesday.

Read Chapter 4. Put the events in order.

a Bella records Alex's song.
b Alex gets four texts from Bella.
c Alex runs to his room and leaves Bella at the door.
d Alex plays one of his songs for Bella.
e Alex calls Bella at seven o'clock in the morning.
f Alex plays the new FLY song for Bella.

At the end of Chapter 4, why is Alex angry? Check (✓) the three reasons.

1 He has to get up early for Bella.
2 Bella didn't ask him before she put the video on VideoSpace.
3 He sang the song for Bella, not for VideoSpace.
4 He doesn't like VideoSpace.
5 He doesn't want people to see the video.
6 Bella is late for her guitar lesson.

Read Chapter 5. Match the quotes with the people.

Alex   Alex's dad   Bella   Miss King   the coolest boy

1 "Is everything OK?" _____
2 "Do you want to come and play your guitar?"
   _____
3 "Do you like this school?" _____
4 "I was wrong." _____
5 "You *have* to come." _____

How many "likes" does Alex have…

1 when the boy with the phone first talks to him?
2 at five o'clock?
3 when Bella looks on VideoSpace after her soccer practice?
4 when Alex and Bella look on his laptop?

Are these sentences true or false?

1 Alex watches the VideoSpace video before he goes to school.
2 There are no bad comments about Alex's song on VideoSpace.
3 The boys in Alex's lesson like his music.
4 Bella texts Alex when she finishes her soccer practice.
5 Alex is never going to put another video on VideoSpace.
6 When Bella kisses Alex, it's his first kiss.

ACTIVITIES: *While Reading*

Read Chapter 6. Match the parts of the sentences.

1 At school, Alex feels really bad because…
2 Alex's mom asks, "Are you happy here?" because…
3 Alex makes a video because…
4 Alex feels good because…

a he wants to say sorry to Bella with a song.
b his mom likes his song.
c she and his dad do not want to move.
d he did not kiss Bella.

What does Alex do in Chapter 6? Write *yes* or *no*.

1 He goes to Bella's house.
2 He talks to his mom about saying sorry.
3 He sings a song about Bella.
4 He sends a VideoSpace link to Bella.
5 He writes a new song.

Read Chapter 7. Choose the correct words to complete the sentences.

claps   is feeling   is smiling   kisses

1 When Alex arrives at the youth club, he _____ sick.
2 When he sees Bella, she _____.
3 When he finishes the song, everyone _____.
4 After the song, Alex _____ Bella.

ACTIVITIES

After Reading

1 **Use the clues below to complete the puzzle with words from the story.**

   1 to think that something is true
   2 a short letter
   3 not well
   4 what you say when you explain why you can't/didn't do something
   5 to answer

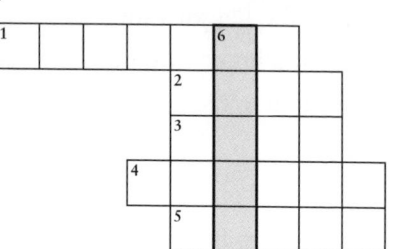

Choose the correct meaning for word 6 in the puzzle.

   a the sound when you speak or sing
   b music with words

2 **Complete the sentences with words from the puzzle in exercise 1.**

   1 She did not want to go out with her friends tonight, so she made an _____, but they didn't _____ her.
   2 I'm not well today, I feel really _____.
   3 Bella texted Alex, but he did not _____.
   4 She left me a _____ on the table: *Goodbye and thank you!*

ACTIVITIES: *After Reading*

Grammar

1 Complete the sentences using the simple present and *-ing* form of the words in parentheses ( ).

Alex _____ (like / watch) music videos.
Alex likes watching music videos.
1 Someone comes to the door, and Alex _____ (stop / play) the guitar.
2 Miss King looks at Alex and _____ (start / talk).
3 Bella _____ (finish / work) and goes next door.
4 They _____ (love / listen) to FLY songs.
5 _____ (stop / sing)! I need to work.

2 Join the sentences using *because* or *so*.

Alex goes out for dinner. It's his birthday.
Alex goes out for dinner because it's his birthday.
1 I can't come to the youth club. I don't like meeting people.
2 Alex likes Bella. He asks her to come and see FLY.
3 Bella runs to school. She's late.
4 Alex wants to say sorry to Bella. He sings her a song.
5 I have a lot of homework. I can't come out tonight.
6 Alex likes Miss King. She's really nice.

Reading

1 Who says these things in the story? Choose the correct person. Then write what they are talking about.

Alex   Alex's mom   Bella   the coolest boy

1 "Is it easy?"
2 "I played this for years."
3 "It's going to be cool."
4 "Is that a new song?"

2 Complete the sentences with words from the story.

Alex does not have many friends because his family is always ¹_____ to different towns. His mom and dad give him a new ²_____ for his ³_____. He plays a song, and Bella, the girl from ⁴_____, hears him. She comes to see him and says, "Can you ⁵_____ me the guitar?"

Bella comes to his house for a ⁶_____ every day. One day, she says, "Can you play me one of your ⁷_____?" She takes a ⁸_____ of him on her phone, and she puts it on VideoSpace.

ACTIVITIES: *After Reading*

Writing

1 Choose the correct words to complete Alex's song.

hear   day   song   away   here   wrong

Everybody is far ¹_____
Only me
Day after ²_____.

Nobody listens and they don't ³_____
Look at me
I'm standing ⁴_____.

Why does everything feel so ⁵_____?
My one friend
Is you, this ⁶_____.

2 Look at the song, and complete the rules below.

1 There are _____ verses, and each verse has _____ lines.
2 In every verse, there are 8 or 9 beats in line 1, _____ beats in line 2, and _____ beats in line 3. (Note: In this song, we say "ev'rybody" and "ev'rything".)
3 In each verse, lines _____ and _____ rhyme.

ACTIVITIES: After Reading

3 **After the music night at the youth club, Alex writes a new song. Unjumble the lines to make three verses, following the rules below. Then put the verses in the best order.**

1 There are five beats in line 1, four beats in line 2, and seven beats in line 3.
2 Lines 1 and 2 rhyme.
3 Line 3 is the same in all three verses.

And I thought: I can do this.
Nothing went wrong,
Looked at the sky,
And I thought: I can do this.
I saw you right there,
I played them my song,
And I thought: I can do this.
I wanted to cry,
Sun in your hair,

4 **Put the words below in rhyming groups.**

away day do free hear here knew me near new see stay through today too true we who year you

be	blue	ear	say

ACTIVITIES: *After Reading* 55

5 Now write two new verses for the song in exercise 3, following the song rules, and using some of the rhyming words in exercise 4. For line 3, you can use the line from verses 1–3 or write a new one.

Speaking

1 What is Alex talking about below? Match the phrases with the words.

being in front of a camera   FLY
his new guitar   his new school   music

¹It's OK.   ²They're amazing.   ³It's really cool.

⁴I don't like it.   ⁵I love it.

2 Write each of the phrases in exercise 1 below the correct picture.

😕	😐	😃

3 Think of one thing that you like or love, one thing that you don't like, and one thing that you think is OK. Then talk about these things with your partner, using the phrases.

ACTIVITIES

Discussion

1 Look at the statement below. Do you agree?

   It was wrong for Bella to put Alex's song on VideoSpace.

2 Which of these sentences do you agree with the most?

   a You must never put a video or picture of someone on a website when they don't know about it.
   b Alex was afraid, and Bella helped him.
   c Alex sang at the youth club, and met some new friends because Bella put his song on VideoSpace.
   d Alex does not like to play for people, and Bella knew that.

3 Discuss the statement in exercise 1 with a partner. Use the words below, the ideas in exercise 2, and your own ideas.

   I agree/disagree with the statement because…
   Yes, but…   That's true, but…

4 Discuss the statements below with your partner. Give reasons for your opinion.

   I don't like it when people have their phones at the dinner table.
   Making time for your family is more important than having lots of money.

Project

1 Look at the pictures and profiles below. Write the people's names in the correct profile.

Brandon Stanton

Rebecca Black

What / name? _____
Where / from? Georgia, USA
How / find fame? Put pictures of people on the streets of New York on a website, *Humans of New York*
When / find fame? 2010
What / do next? Wrote a book in 2015; went around the world taking more pictures for the website

What / name? _____
Where / from? California, USA
How / find fame? Put a pop song called *Friday* and a video on a website
When / find fame? 2011
What / do next? Went on TV; sang *Saturday* in 2013

2 Read the profiles again and answer the questions. Are they true or false?

1 Brandon Stanton is from New York.
2 He took pictures of people on the streets.
3 He found fame in 2010.
4 He stopped taking pictures after he wrote his book.
5 Rebecca Black is from California.
6 Her first song was about the weekend.
7 She found fame in 2013.
8 She went on TV and sang another song.

3 Complete the questions in the profile of Brandon Stanton. Then answer the questions.

1 What *is* / *has* his name?
2 Where *does* / *is* he from?
3 How *did* / *does* he find fame?
4 When *was* / *did* he find fame?
5 What *did* / *does* he do next?

4 Write questions to ask about Rebecca Black. Use the prompts to help.

1 What / name?
2 Where / from?
3 How / find fame?
4 When / find fame?
5 What / do next?

5 Work with a partner. Take turns to ask and answer the questions about Rebecca Black.

6 Find information about a different person who found fame on a website. Complete a profile about the person.

| What / name? |
| Where / from? |
| How / find fame? |
| When / find fame? |
| What / do next? |

7 Work with a partner. Ask and answer questions about the person in exercise 6. Show a picture or video.

8 Speak to other students. How many of the famous people are:

   men   women   from the USA   singers   famous now

9 Speak to other students. Would you like to find fame on a website? Why/Why not?

THE OXFORD BOOKWORMS LIBRARY

THE OXFORD BOOKWORMS LIBRARY is a best-selling series of graded readers which provides authentic and enjoyable reading in English. It includes a wide range of original and adapted texts: classic and modern fiction, non-fiction, and plays. There are more than 250 Bookworms to choose from, in seven carefully graded language stages that go from beginner to advanced level.

Each Bookworm is illustrated, and offers extensive support, including:

- a glossary of above-level words
- activities to develop language and communication skills
- notes about the author and story
- online tests

Each Bookworm pack contains a reader and audio.

6	**STAGE 6**	2500 HEADWORDS	CEFR B2–C1
5	**STAGE 5**	1800 HEADWORDS	CEFR B2
4	**STAGE 4**	1400 HEADWORDS	CEFR B1–B2
3	**STAGE 3**	1000 HEADWORDS	CEFR B1
2	**STAGE 2**	700 HEADWORDS	CEFR A2–B1
1	**STAGE 1**	400 HEADWORDS	CEFR A1–A2
S	**STARTER**	250 HEADWORDS	CEFR A1

Find a full list of *Bookworms* and resources at
www.oup.com/elt/gradedreaders

If you liked this Bookworm, why not try...

One-Way-Ticket – short stories
JENNIFER BASSETT

Tom liked the two girls on the train. Tom thought they were nice and friendly and fun. Tom certainly had a lot to learn about life...

This is a collection of short stories about adventures on trains.